D0793603

ETHICS OF SPORTS

Getting Ahead:

Drugs, Technology, and Competitive Advantage

Lori Hile

Heinemann Library
Chicago, Illinois

an imprint of Capstone Global Library, LLC
Chicago, Illinois

Edited by Adrian Vigliano and Claire Throp
Designed by Richard Parker
Original illustrations © Capstone Global Ltd 2012
Illustrations by Darren Lingard
Picture research by Ruth Blair
Originated by Capstone Global Library Ltd
Printed in the United States of America in North Mankato, Minnesota.

15 14 13
10 9 8 7 6 5 4 3

Library of Congress Cataloging-in-Publication Data
Hile, Lori.
Getting ahead : drugs, technology, and the competitive advantage / Lori Hile.
p. cm.—(Ethics of sports)
Includes bibliographical references and index.
ISBN 978-1-4329-5978-4 (hb)—ISBN 978-1-4329-5983-8 (pb) 1. Sports—Moral and ethical aspects. 2. Doping in sports. I. Title.
GV706.3.H55 2012
174.9796—dc22 2011014609

032013
007187RP

Acknowledgments
We would like to thank the following for permission to reproduce photographs: Corbis pp. 8 (© Reix - Liewig/For Picture), 10 (© Reuters), 11 (© Jerry Lampen/Reuters), 18 (© Mathieu Belanger/Reuters), 20 (© Gilbert Iundt; Jean-Yves Ruszniewski/TempSport), 39 (© AM/TDWsport.com), 41 (© Wang Lei/Xinhua Press), 45 (© Leo Mason), 50 (© Rick Rickman/NewSport), 52 (© Bo Bridges), 53 (© Greg Ashman/ZUMA Press); Getty Images pp. 13 (Ross Kinnaird), 15 (Archive Holdings Inc.), 16 (Robert Decelis Ltd), 29 (Streeter Lecka), 31 (Ben Radford/ALLSPORT), 33 (Doug Pensinger), 37 (Richard Mackson/Sports Illustrated), 44 (Andy Lyons); PA Photos pp. 19 (AP Photo/Alessandra Tarantino), 47; Science Photo Library pp. 35 (Sheila Terry), 49 (Lawrence Lawry); Shutterstock pp. 4 (© Jamie Robinson), 6 (© Sportsphotographer.eu), 21 (© Phil Date), 43 (© Amy Myers).

Cover photograph of a cyclist reproduced with permission of Getty Images (Feng Li).

We would like to thank Shawn E. Klein for his invaluable help in the preparation of this book.

CONTENTS

Some words are printed in bold, **like this**. You can find out what they mean by looking in the glossary.

HIGHER! FASTER! STRONGER!

The Olympic track stadium is packed. The 200-meter race is about to start, and you have the best seat in the house. You watch as the runners shake out their legs before the big race. Your favorite sprinter's face is focused, and her muscles are flexed. The gun goes off. In a split second, your runner is far ahead of the pack. She leads, first by a head, then by the length of a body, as she zooms past the finish line in record-breaking time. You are ecstatic.

But a few days later, you learn that your track star ran so fast partly because she was taking **steroids**. She is disqualified from the race for having an unfair competitive advantage. You vow never to watch her again. What she did was so unfair!

Young people may feel a lot of pressure from coaches and parents to do well in sports. Maintaining a balance in life is also important, however.

The ethics of sports

"It's so unfair!" is a statement about **ethics**, or standards of conduct. Acting **ethically** is, simply put, doing the right thing. Sports ethics are about doing the right thing in sports. Sometimes it seems obvious what is fair and what is not fair. Maybe you see a goalie blocking a goal—after it crossed the goal line. Or perhaps you watch a tennis ball bounce inside the line, only to have the umpire call it out.

But sometimes we get such mixed messages from parents, coaches, political leaders, and peers that it is difficult to know just what the right thing is. For instance, we may be told that "drugs are bad," only to be bombarded with magazine articles or ads telling us how different drugs can magically cure everything from sleep problems to weight gain to social anxiety. Sometimes, even when we know what the "right" thing is, we find it difficult to follow through.

Doing the right, or ethical, thing is different than following laws and rules. For instance, there is no "law" against cheating on tests, something most people would consider **unethical**. Sometimes even rules or laws can be unethical. For instance, some people believe that drug testing for athletes is unethical because it is an invasion of privacy (see pages 38 and 39).

The competitive advantage

One reason people do things that are unethical, like cheating on tests—or races—is to get ahead. People sometimes break the rules, or at least bend them, so they can look smarter or perform better than their competitors. The desire to get ahead is human. Since most sports involve competition, athletes often feel this desire more than anyone.

Athletes may also feel a lot of pressure—from coaches, fans, **sponsors**, and the **media**—to perform at a high level. Over the last 100 years, sports have grown from an amusing pastime into big business. Sports teams, stars, equipment companies, television stations, and vendors all rake in lots of money from sporting events. To stay in the game, athletes look for an edge.

There is nothing wrong with achieving a competitive advantage in sports. Without it, there would never be a winner—or a superstar. If everyone performed at exactly the same level, there would be lots of boring—and tied—games! But it is important to consider how this advantage is achieved.

Facing limitations

The motto of the Olympic Games is: "Faster, Higher, Stronger!" Athletes are not only expected to run fast, but to run faster than ever before. They are not only expected to jump high, but to jump higher than ever before. They are not only expected to be strong, but to be stronger than ever before. But people do not often quote the founding idea of the Olympics: "The essential [most important] thing is not to have won, but to have fought well."[1]

The human body has limitations. Even with natural talent, rigorous training, and specialized diets, athletes can only run so fast, jump so high, and become so strong. Faced with these limitations, how can athletes continue to break records and entertain the masses?

New technologies have raised the bar on sports. From shoes to the materials used to make the high jump bar, advances have helped to produce higher jumps, faster sprints, and longer throws.

For many athletes, the answer lies in technology. Cutting-edge sports clothing and equipment can help athletes run and ski faster than ever, hit farther, and jump higher (see pages 8 to 17). Many athletes also turn to drugs or **nutritional supplements**. **Anabolic steroids** (see pages 20 to 29) and other **performance-enhancing drugs** (see pages 30 to 35) can help make athletes bigger and stronger than ever before. Some athletes may even consider more radical methods, like altering their **genes** (see pages 46 to 49), in the hopes of gaining super-human strength.

Questions arise

While technology and drugs may help athletes shatter records, they also raise many ethical questions. For instance, when does technology give an athlete too much of a boost, making the game too easy and his or her own accomplishments too small? Do the benefits of steroids ever outweigh the harmful side effects? And why do many people consider it wrong to take steroids, but acceptable to take other nutritional supplements or products that may produce similar results?

The answers to these questions are not always clear. Unlike laws or rules, which outline specific guidelines for conduct, ethics are not as simple. Many people disagree on what exactly is fair, but almost everyone agrees that we should strive for fairness and honesty both on and off the sports field. Some people say that sports, since they are played in the public eye, should in fact be a model for the very best of human behavior—both physically and ethically. The sports arena is certainly a good place to consider questions of fairness. We can watch rules as they are broken and decide whether new ones are needed.

This book will help you do just that. You will see how changes in technology and performance-enhancing drugs are helping athletes gain a competitive advantage. You will find arguments both defending and opposing these changes. After considering all of these different viewpoints and questions, you can begin to determine for yourself just what the right thing is, as you watch a game or find yourself playing one. Then, you just have to do it!

"All I know most surely about morality and obligations, I owe to football [soccer]."

Albert Camus, Nobel Prize-winning French writer and philosopher; former goalkeeper for the University of Algiers[2]

TECHNOLOGY: A GAME CHANGER

	Sprinter Jesse Owens		Sprinter Usain Bolt
Who:	Sprinter Jesse Owens	**Who**:	Sprinter Usain Bolt
When:	1936	**When**:	2009
Where:	Summer Olympics, Berlin, Germany	**Where**:	World Championships, Berlin, Germany
What:	100-meter race	**What**:	100-meter race
Finish time:	10.3 seconds, tying a world record	**Finish time**:	9.58 seconds, a new world record
What:	200-meter race	**What**:	200-meter race
Finish time:	20.7 seconds, a world record[1]	**Finish time**:	19.19 seconds, a new world record[2]

Jesse Owens and Usain Bolt are two amazing athletes from two different time periods. They also had different finish times. So, who's the better athlete? Judging by speed alone, Bolt would be the winner. But not so fast! When comparing athletes from different time periods, many factors play a role, including the use of technology.

Sprinter Usain Bolt broke two world records in 2009. Will new technologies help someone break his records?

Consider the resources Usain Bolt likely has available to him, which Jesse Owens did not: springier, more **aerodynamic** shoes; more advanced training techniques; and a diet informed by a better understanding of nutrition. Consider, too, that the technology used to time races is much more precise today. When Owens ran, he was timed by six men with stopwatches.[3] Three of these watches recorded a longer time than the others. It is the slower times that made the record books. Bolt's finish was recorded by state-of-the-art equipment. In races, every split second counts.

Now who do you think is the better athlete? While it is impossible to ever know for sure, it is true that most athletes today perform at higher levels than athletes in the past. As technology evolves and improves, so do sports and athletes. With innovations such as better running shoes, equipment, and training facilities, athletes regularly smash records set by athletes decades ago and set new standards for performance in sports.

THE TECHNOLOGY OF TENNIS RACKETS

In many cases, the competitive advantage provided by technology has revolutionized the way that games are played, creating new standards for achievement. These technology upgrades have been game changers. This has been true as tennis rackets have changed over time.

In 1983 Swedish tennis star Björn Borg shocked the tennis world when he announced his retirement at the age of 26. In 1991 Borg tried to stage a comeback, using his old wooden racket. Unfortunately, he was pummeled by a little-known player, who was using a newer graphite racket.[4] Was Borg's wooden racket to blame? Or was Borg simply past his prime (or out of practice)? Either way, most players today only use graphite rackets, which are much lighter and more long-lasting than the old, wooden variety. Without the new racket, a player would be at a significant disadvantage.

Many technological innovations are welcome, since they raise the level of competition and keep audiences on the edge of their seats. But the competitive advantages offered by technology also raise ethical questions. For instance, what will happen if technology hits a limit? Some athletic shoe companies, for example, believe that their shoes are about as good as they will ever be. If athletes no longer break records, will fans lose interest? Also, by helping athletes run faster and jump higher, can technology be dangerous for athletes?

Clothing and equipment design

In September 2010, an innovative sports clothing and equipment company rolled out new sneakers. The sneakers use a rubber springlike device to help launch players an extra 3 inches (7.6 centimeters) into the air when they jump. In October 2010, the shoes, called the Concept 1, were officially banned by the National Basketball Association (NBA).[5] The NBA's stated reason was: "Under league rules, players may not wear any shoe during a game that creates an undue competitive advantage."[6] Most people can agree that spring-loaded shoes might provide players who wear them an unfair "lift"—or, worse, turn the sport into a sort of circus. But many other cases involving clothing are not as clear-cut.

Swim like a shark

Scientists have studied sharks, the world's fastest swimmers. Speedo, a swimsuit company, used scientists' observations when designing a bodysuit for swimmers. Called Fastskin, the suit consists of a series of textured panels that repel (push away) water and move in sections, like a shark's skin.[7] Swimmers who tested the bodysuit found that it shaved valuable seconds off their times.

Fastskin bodysuits, developed to mimic the motions of sharks, are so effective that they have been banned from swim competitions for offering an unfair advantage.

But many people argue that the suit provides an unfair advantage. An Italian coach even called the suit a kind of "technical doping."[8] The main objection to the suit has to do with sponsors. Most top swimmers are "sponsored," or given money by clothing companies in return for wearing the company's clothes and promoting its products. Many athletes rely on this money for training. The problem with the bodysuit is that its technology is **patented**, or owned, only by Speedo. It is illegal for other swimsuit companies to copy the suits. Swimmers sponsored by these other companies are not able to wear the bodysuits. In 2010, it was decided that all swimmers should be banned from wearing the bodysuit until other companies offer equally effective technology, and it became illegal to wear the suits in competition.[9]

Artificial legs, artificial speed?

Most people would think that having no legs would put an athlete at a competitive disadvantage, not an advantage, in qualifying as an Olympic runner. The International Association of Athletics Federations (IAAF) thought otherwise. In 2008, the IAAF barred South African runner Oscar Pistorius, who lost both of his legs as a baby, from competing in the 2008 Beijing Olympics. They said that the metal blades that Pistorius attaches to his knees offer him a "clear competitive advantage" over runners with natural legs. They based their decision on tests that showed that Pistorius was able to run at the same speed as other runners while using a quarter less energy.

Pistorius challenged the decision, arguing that his carbon-fiber blades simply offered him the same opportunity to run as able-bodied athletes. The Court of Arbitration for Sport agreed, and it reversed the decision. In the end, Pistorius did not run fast enough to qualify for the Games.

Oscar Pistorius argued that the blades he uses could put him at a disadvantage by making him lose traction on wet tracks.

Many athletes look to technology for advantages in the equipment they use. Consider these examples.

Ultralight cycles

Track cyclists fly around specially built indoor tracks, called velodromes, at speeds of up to 45 miles per hour (72 kilometers per hour).[10] The lighter the bike, the faster the racer goes. Technology has helped create bicycles so light that racers can move more efficiently over long distances. The International Cycling Union (UCI), however, has banned the use of ultralight bicycles weighing under 15 pounds (6.8 kilograms) in competition.[11]

The first reason they cite is "unequal access." These super-high-tech bikes can cost more than $100,000, making them unaffordable to many cyclists. This, they say, would provide an unfair competitive advantage to the few racers who can afford the bikes. Opponents of the ban argue that access to performance-enhancing technology is never equal, anyway. They argue that some cyclists already have better access to top coaches, training programs, or facilities—yet these things are not banned.[12]

The second reason cited for the ban on ultralight bikes is a concern that the effectiveness of the bicycles would focus more attention on the equipment than on the athlete.[13] In other words, fans might be more awed by the superfast bikes than by the athletes riding them.

SOMETHING FISHY

In 2006 a small company in Connecticut first sold a fishing lure so real that it fooled both fish and fishers. Called the KickTail, the lure mimics the movements of tiny fish called minnows. It does this so effectively that eight fishers could not tell the difference between the lure and real minnows when the lure "swam." Plus, fishers sing the lures caught three times as many fish in an hour as fishers using other lures or even live bait. The lures are so successful that they were banned in fishing contests in which live bait is prohibited.[14] Some say this penalizes the company that developed them, since equipment companies rely on promotion at tournaments. But others agree that using a product this realistic would be cheating.

The Superman position

It's a bird, it's a plane, it's Graeme Obree! In 1995 Scottish track cyclist Graeme Obree, also known as "The Flying Scotsman," took the cycling world by storm when he invented a new cycling position. With his body hunched forward and his arms stretched out straight in front of him, resting on a long, narrow set of handlebars, Obree looked like Superman flying through the air as he flew around the oval track. Soon other cyclists adopted the so-called "Superman position" and found that this streamlined stance helped them go faster. Obree's innovation, however, was banned by the UCI in 1996 because it was considered "too aerodynamic."[15]

"Flying Scotsman" Graeme Obree's low-tech, low-cost "Superman position" was banned because it was said to offer cyclists too great an advantage.

The decision has been debated.[16] Many cyclists complain that the ban simply encourages cyclists to look for more high-tech ways to achieve an aerodynamic advantage. Cyclists, for instance, spend time in wind tunnels trying to find the best legal position. This is extremely expensive and will probably result in an even greater competitive advantage than the low-cost, low-tech Superman position. It also puts cyclists with less money at a disadvantage.

Does technology make us safer, or does it put us at greater risk? It helps us jump higher, run faster, and play harder than ever before. But the higher we jump, the farther we can fall. Does safety technology also encourage athletes to take more dangerous risks?

Ski technology

If you wanted to go downhill skiing in 1940, you would clip the toe of your boots to long wooden slats. Then you could speed down a slope at 40 miles per hour (64 kilometers per hour). But skiers began tinkering with ski equipment in an attempt to reduce friction (rubbing) between the skis and snow. As ski materials evolved from wood to plastic to fiberglass, skiing speeds increased to 80 miles per hour (129 kilometers per hour) over 60 years.

But the increased speeds also increased the number of severe injuries. Now, instead of isolated **ligament** injuries, multiple ligament injuries are more likely. Instead of simple fractures, there are complex bone fractures.[17] Modern medical technology means that doctors can more efficiently treat bone fractures. But the dangers of skiing still raise the question: Just because we have the technology to do something, should we always use it, even if it puts our bodies at risk?

Helmets: A false sense of security?

Football and **rugby** can be brutal. Both involve tackling opponents to gain advantage of the ball. But only football players wear a helmet. Does this make football safer than rugby?

Modern football helmets made of plastic and Styrofoam were designed mainly to prevent serious injuries such as skull fractures (broken skulls). However, modern helmets do not prevent **concussions**.[18] Some long-term consequences of repeated concussions can include long-term memory loss, clinical depression, and increased odds of losing many mental functions at an early age.[19]

Players wearing bulky pads and thick helmets tend to feel **invincible**, so they often use their heads to ram into the helmets of opposing players (even though this is officially against the rules). Unfortunately, football players are not invincible. Not only do helmets do nothing to stop concussions, but they also do nothing to prevent serious neck injuries, which can lead to **paralysis**—or death.

Early football helmets did little to protect players from serious head injuries, but they may have helped discourage players from making dangerous tackles.

The National Football League (NFL) is taking steps to research concussions and develop new helmets to prevent them. But most of these helmets are large and heavy, which could interfere with a player's ability to play. The NFL has also begun enforcing a rule that prevents players from launching into the head of players who are in the act of throwing or catching a ball.[20] But many NFL players object to the rule.

Some doctors and sports experts have proposed getting rid of the helmet altogether, like football's cousin, rugby. Without helmets, they argue, players would be forced to tone down their tackles. Instead of hitting opponents with their heads, rugby players are taught to tackle opponents by wrapping their bodies around them.[21] But many football players and fans argue that part of football's appeal is its explosive hits. Playing without helmets might make football safer, but would the game still be football?

Training tools

In the 1985 movie *Rocky IV*, the short, wiry U.S. boxer Rocky Balboa takes on the bulging, blond Russian boxer Ivan Drago. Drago has a team of scientists and a room full of high-tech equipment. He is continuously monitored by multiple trainers and injected with anabolic steroids. Rocky's training regimen, on the other hand, is completely low-tech. He throws logs, chops down trees, jogs in thick snow, and climbs mountains. In the end, Rocky is the victor, winning the good, old-fashioned way.

In reality, Sylvester Stallone, the actor playing Rocky, was groomed for the role by a team of trainers using high-tech equipment. Many believe that he was also taking performance-enhancing drugs at the time.[22] The United States and other Western countries often romanticize rugged, old-fashioned methods for winning, and they depict the use of technology or science as a form of cheating. But in truth, most Western countries use and develop some of the most cutting-edge methods for training.

High-tech computers can record every move a body makes. This information is used to help skaters and other athletes achieve their best possible performance.

The ethics of high-tech training

As proud as fans may be of the cutting-edge technology available to athletes, they also seem suspicious of it. Why would we rather see our athletes hauling logs than hooked to high-tech monitors? The following factors may play a role:

- *Cost*: High-tech equipment is very expensive. This places athletes or countries that cannot afford expensive technology at a competitive disadvantage. It also raises the question: Are teams or athletes who train with high-tech devices "buying" victory?
- *Is training fair?*: Just 100 years ago, the idea of training itself was sometimes viewed as an unfair advantage. Today, training is so commonplace among both amateurs and professionals that it would be considered bad conduct to enter a meet without it. But some people believe that the scale has tipped too far and that many young athletes are putting too much emphasis on competition and training and not enough on enjoyment. After all, games are supposed to involve "play," not just "work."
- *Individualism*: As technology becomes such a dominant force in sports, many people worry that sports will become a showcase for the talent of a team of scientists, rather than for an athlete's unique skills.
- *Fear of technology and change*: Technology dominates our lives, yet science fiction movies and books often depict technology as scary and dangerous to humans. It is always "man versus machine," not "man and machine." Some people fear that technology will eventually replace the "human" element in sports.

Biomechanics

One cutting-edge method is **biomechanics**. This is a form of science that studies how the muscles, bones, and other parts of the body work together to help humans achieve the best possible performance. Scientists observe professional swimmers, basketball players, and other athletes and put their movements into digital (computerized) form (see photograph on page 16). This way, their movements can be replayed and analyzed, frame-by-frame, to determine which ones enhance their performance and which ones hinder it.[23] These observations can help individual athletes improve their game and also help trainers develop strategies to raise the level of play in the sport as a whole.

Instant replay

Originally, television was simply a way for people to watch games they could not attend. But after stations began broadcasting "instant replays" for viewers, many sports leagues decided to adopt the technology to ensure accurate calls. Today, most professional sports leagues use instant replay, including basketball, hockey, rugby, cricket, and many tennis tournaments.

Like many other sports leagues, the National Hockey League uses instant replay to review controversial goals.

The two major sports that most resist using instant replay technology are baseball and soccer. In baseball, opponents of instant replay point to the sport's long tradition. In order to accurately compare statistics between past and present players, they argue that conditions should remain the same. Also, just as players sometimes make errors, they argue, so do umpires. This makes the game human and relatable, rather than mechanical.

People who support instant replay in baseball argue that many factors have changed over the years, including equipment and diet. Since we have the technology, they believe we owe it to players to make sure that calls are as fair as possible.

In soccer, opponents have argued that technology is not 100 percent foolproof and that checking instant replay cameras significantly slows down the game. But there is talk of using a "smartball" loaded with a computer chip. The chip would track the ball's precise position in real time, including when or if it has fully passed the goal line. That information would be relayed to a referee in less than a second.[24]

Role of the athlete

Others say that the people who know best what takes place in a game are the players themselves. They believe that if athletes took more responsibility, we would not require so much technology.

Philosopher Peter Singer cites the example of a 2010 soccer World Cup game between England and Germany, in which instant replay clearly showed that England had scored a goal. Unfortunately, the referee had already blown the call, and game rules prevented a reversal. Singer argues that the German goalkeeper, Manuel Neuer, should have told the referee that it was actually a goal.[25] Others argue that this kind of honesty is simply not realistic, especially since fans demand "wins" from their teams as much or more so than fair play. They believe that only technology will help keep athletes honest.

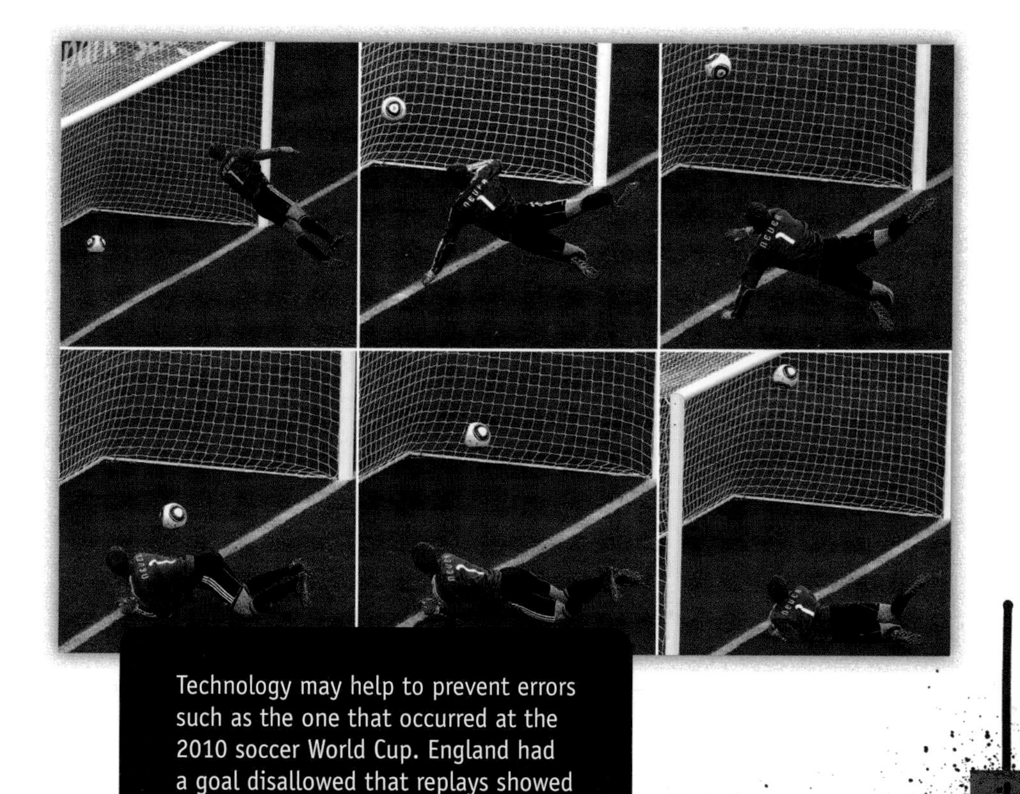

Technology may help to prevent errors such as the one that occurred at the 2010 soccer World Cup. England had a goal disallowed that replays showed had actually gone over the line.

STEROIDS: IS BIGGER BETTER?

If you were offered a magic pill that would guarantee you would win a gold medal in the Olympics, would you take it? When asked this question, 100 percent of Olympic-level athletes said "yes." Now, what if you were offered a pill that would guarantee you a gold medal, but . . . you would die from its harmful side effects just five years later? Would you still take it? More than 50 percent of top athletes still said "yes!"[1]

It seems that many athletes would do almost anything to get ahead. But just as the human body has its limits, so does technology. When technology can no longer offer athletes the edge they need, many people turn to performance-enhancing drugs—so-called "magic pills." Steroids are just one kind of performance-enhancing drug, but they are one of the best known—and most dangerous. Steroids have been illegal in the Olympics since 1976, when tests were first carried out, and are banned by the **World Anti-Doping Agency (WADA)** as well as almost every sports league and team in the world. But that has not stopped some athletes from using them.

Lewis v. Johnson

One of the most dramatic examples of steroid use, or "doping," in sports occurred at the 1988 Summer Olympic Games in Seoul, South Korea. Canadian sprinter Ben Johnson zipped past U.S. runner and longtime rival Carl Lewis in the 100-meter race, in a world-record 9.79 seconds. Lewis finished second, at 9.92 seconds. But just three days later, Johnson was disqualified after testing positive for stanozolol, an anabolic steroid. He was stripped of his medal, which was then awarded to Lewis.

The continued presence of steroids in sports raises a number of ethical questions, such as: Does steroid use violate the spirit of sports? Or does it simply reflect a "win-at-all-costs" mindset common in sports? Why are some technologies considered acceptable, while drugs are not? A look at steroids may shed light on these questions.

What are steroids?

Steroids are substances that resemble **testosterone**, the male sex **hormone** responsible for the growth of the male reproductive organs as well as muscles and bone mass. Women naturally have testosterone, too, but in much smaller amounts. Steroids are **synthetic**, meaning that they are created in a laboratory.

Hundreds of different steroids have been made, all with slightly different effects. The steroid **cortisone** treats illnesses or injuries. Anabolic steroids, the kind most commonly used by athletes, build muscle. They can be swallowed as a tablet or injected into the body as a liquid.[2]

Steroids remain in the body several weeks after being injected. They can help speed the rate of muscle growth, but they can also be harmful. Steroids are also worthless without exercise.

Steroids are not magic pills. If your average couch potato took steroids, he or she would not instantly look like a bulging bodybuilder. But with strenuous workouts and a high-protein diet, steroids can help build muscles and reduce the amount of time it takes for athletes to recover between workouts. It is unclear, however, whether steroids actually increase muscle strength. Bigger muscles do not necessarily mean stronger muscles.[3]

Health risks

To build bigger muscles, athletes take steroids in much larger doses than what is considered safe by doctors. This leads to harmful side effects. But it is difficult for scientists to fully understand these effects. This is because scientists consider it unethical to give humans doses this large in order to study the potential side effects. Even if athletes currently using steroids agreed to be tested, ethics committees would never approve such a study. However, even at low levels, steroids have been shown to pose major health risks (see the diagram below).

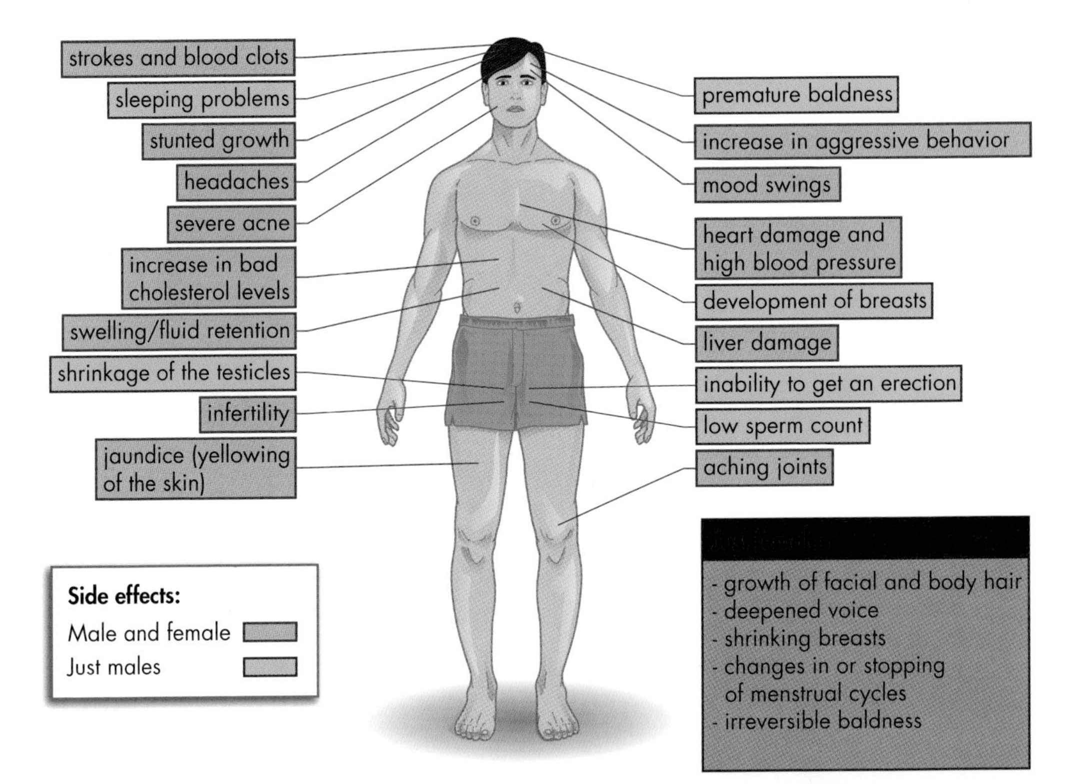

In males, many of the side effects of using steroids appear to stop once the steroid use has stopped. In females, however, many side effects appear to be irreversible.

Some doctors believe that small doses of steroids may be safe for adult males, but others disagree. Some also believe that small doses have no benefits. One thing doctors agree on is that large doses of steroids are always dangerous. Steroids, even in small doses, are always dangerous for young people and women. Steroids can make women **infertile**, a side effect that cannot be reversed. Unlike almost all other drugs, the harmful effects of steroids might not be seen for months, years, or even decades after taking them.[4]

Real world stories

In addition to the documented side effects, high doses of steroids have been linked to cancers and premature deaths. For instance, many professional wrestlers, including Eddie Guerrero and Davey Boy Smith have died of heart failure believed to be due to long-term steroid use. In World Wrestling Entertainment (WWE), wrestlers are dying at six times the rate of other people, most of them from heart disease.[5]

Why athletes take steroids

Athletes generally take steroids in the hopes that they will improve their athletic ability. But given the potential risks, why do some athletes still use them? Here are some reasons given by users:

- Since sports careers are generally short, athletes face a limited window of opportunity. Many athletes believe that steroids will help them achieve success more quickly.
- Many athletes believe the harms of steroids are exaggerated.
- Some athletes believe that "everybody takes them," and so to remain competitive they must, too.
- Many athletes feel pressure from coaches and trainers to take the drugs to help give their team a competitive advantage or to achieve a better position on their team.
- Once athletes begin taking steroids, the "high" they get from them may become addictive. Some feel depressed after discontinuing use.
- Many believe that the potential side effects will not happen to them.

There is no "typical" steroid user among athletes. Users include more men than women, but there is an equal percentage of rich and poor and different races.[6] Anonymous surveys among professional U.S. powerlifters showed that as many as 66 percent used steroids, as well as more than 33 percent of U.S. women athletes training at gyms. International numbers are estimated to be similar for sports that require speed and strength.[7] Steroid users have been found in every single sport.

Teenagers and performance-enhancing drugs

Increasingly, teenage athletes are feeling pressure from high-school coaches, Olympic trainers, and college or professional teams to "get bigger" or "get faster" in order to get ahead. To cope with increasingly intense workouts and long seasons, some teenagers are turning to steroids and other performance-enhancing drugs to boost their strength and energy levels.

Taylor Hooton and the pressure to "get bigger"

Sixteen-year-old Plano, Texas, teenager Taylor Hooton was a talented high school baseball player. He longed to be his varsity team's top pitcher, but one of his coaches told him that he needed to get "bigger" to be considered. Since the coach never suggested a workout regimen or training plan, Hooton found his own method for increasing his size: taking steroids, which he bought illegally at a gym near his home.

At 6 feet, 2 inches (188 centimeters) tall and 180 pounds (82 kilograms), Hooton was hardly small. But the steroids did help him bulk up. He gained nearly 30 pounds (13 kilograms) after taking steroids and began lifting 100-pound (45-kilogram) weights with ease. However, the steroids also changed his behavior—he became more aggressive. He began yelling, pounding on tables, and hitting walls, something he had never done before. A doctor took him off the steroids and prescribed medication to deal with any depression he might encounter from the withdrawal. A few weeks later, at the age of 17, Hooton hanged himself.[8]

What exactly led to Hooton's death? His parents blame the steroids, and they have made it their mission to educate other families about the dangers. But the finger could also be pointed at Hooton's school or coach, who encouraged him to "get big" without outlining a healthy plan to guide him. Also, Hooton's parents did not even realize he had been taking steroids. Some doctors believe that Taylor might have already been depressed and began taking the steroids as a way to raise his self-esteem. If nothing else, Hooton's tragic death draws attention to steroid use among teens and shows how many factors may contribute to it.

Since the early 1980s, teenage steroid use has increased, although it began leveling off in 2007. In the United States, one survey shows that nearly half a million adolescents have tried steroids.[9] Rates in countries such as Canada, Australia, Britain, and Sweden appear to be similar, especially among young males.[10]

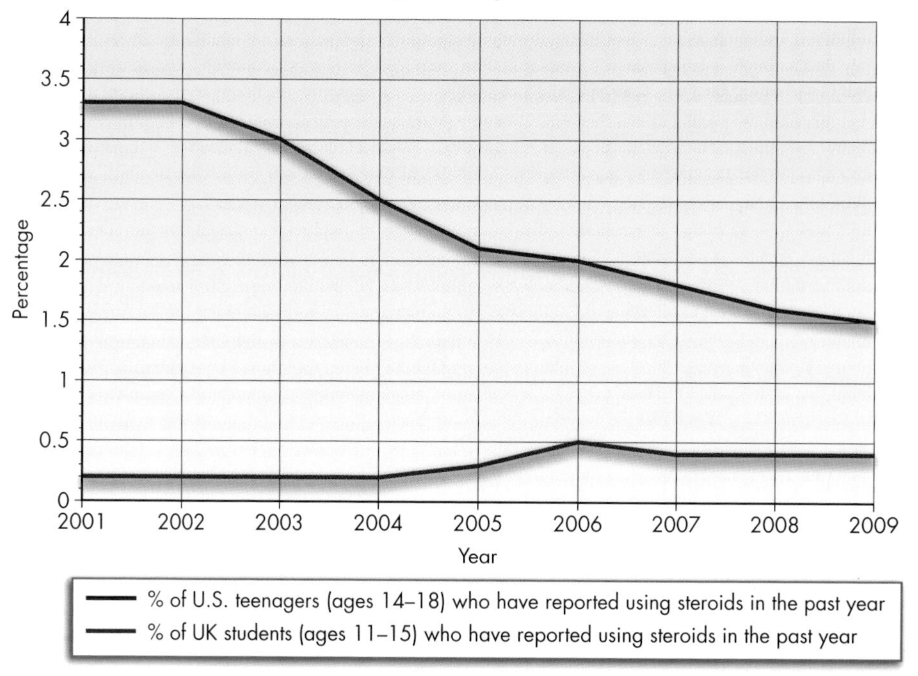

Many popular U.S. sports require size and strength, which may explain the higher U.S. numbers shown on this graph. Recent bans, increased drug testing, and an increase in the awareness of harms may explain the recent drop. The UK has seen recent increases in steroid use among teens hoping to enhance their body image.

Most teenagers can easily buy steroids, yet they present even more dangers for teenagers than adults. Here's why:

- Teenagers often feel invincible. Since they are young, many believe they will never get sick or die.
- The regions of the brain that restrain risky behavior are not fully developed until age 25. This means that teenagers and young adults may engage in more impulsive and potentially dangerous actions.
- Teenagers taking steroids generally do not have access to doctors, who might help regulate their use of drugs.
- Since steroids are a synthetic form of testosterone, the body slows down its natural production of testosterone when steroids are used. Since teenage bodies need natural testosterone to grow, steroids often end up stunting their growth and muscle development.
- Many teenagers are uneducated about the harmful side effects of steroids.
- Steroids may be a "gateway" to other drugs such as heroin, cocaine, or ecstasy. Teenagers can obtain these drugs from their steroid "dealers" and use them to curb feelings of aggression, anxiety, or **insomnia** that result from steroid use.

The ethics of steroid use

There is little doubt that steroids can be harmful. But "harmful" is not the same thing as "wrong." After all, simply playing sports can be harmful to one's health! Is using steroids simply dangerous—or is it also unfair?

In the 1990s and early 2000s, Major League Baseball saw a big increase in home runs. Superstars such as Sammy Sosa, Mark McGwire, and Barry Bonds all broke home run records, but they also broke rules. All three of them later admitted to using steroids and other performance-enhancing drugs to help them achieve their amazing feats.

Many fans felt betrayed when they heard this news, and they even called the athletes' accomplishments into question. For instance, even though Mark McGwire has hit the second-highest number of home runs in baseball history, he has not yet been voted into the Baseball Hall of Fame, for which he is eligible. Many believe that this reflects the public's unhappiness with his steroid use. Many fans also believe that these "steroid era" players should have asterisks (*) put next to their records, to indicate that these records were achieved with the help of performance-enhancing drugs.[12]

Is using steroids "cheating?"

Fans are frustrated not because these players might have harmed themselves using steroids. They are upset that these players might have harmed the game or their own accomplishments. Is using steroids cheating?

In the simplest sense, yes. Steroids and other performance-enhancing drugs have been banned by the WADA, the Olympics, and sports leagues in most countries. They can legally be obtained only by prescription for the treatment of certain diseases. So, using steroids to enhance performance is cheating. But what is the reason for the bans in the first place? Are authorities concerned about players' safety—or is there something fundamentally unfair about using steroids?

The bottom line is this. Steroid use can be fair if all athletes have the opportunity to use them. But this would also cancel out the competitive advantage they offer. Many people argue that steroids harm both the athlete and the value of his or her accomplishments. For arguments both for and against steroid use, see the chart on the next page.

Using steroids is unfair	Using steroids is fair
Robbing "clean" athletes of money and dreams	
Many people believe that steroid users are cheating "clean" athletes out of their dreams, not to mention the money that winning can generate. Steroid use can also make fans suspicious of "clean" athletes who accomplish amazing feats.	Allowing steroid use for everyone would mean that no one would cheat anyone out of anything. It would also remove any reason for fans to accuse players of cheating.
Unfair advantage	
Steroid use gives an unfair competitive advantage to athletes who use them.	Steroid use is only unfair if players do not have equal access to the drugs. If steroids were permitted, anyone could gain the same advantage.
Too easy	
Steroids make athletic accomplishments too easy, and the athlete's role in these accomplishments is too small.	How do steroids differ from other forms of technology that enhance performance, such as bicycles? Also, steroids do not guarantee victory. Even with steroids, an athlete must employ hard work and talent to win.
Human robots?	
Unlike technology, steroids actually change the chemistry of the athlete's body. They blur the line between the athlete's own skill and strength and that which is a result of the steroids.	Other substances change the body, too, such as protein. But no one thinks that protein shakes are "wrong." Where do you draw the line between which substances are good at enhancing performance and which ones are "too good?"
Bad example for youth	
Steroid use by athletes sets a bad example for teenagers, who want to be like their sports idols.	Athletes should not be role models. Steroid use sets a bad example only if it is bad, which has not been proven.
Harming the spirit of sports	
Steroid use violates the spirit of sports, which is about fair play, not winning at all costs.	The sports industry values winning. It is unfair to reward athletes for winning, but to penalize them for using a proven method for achieving success.
Steroids are harmful	
Athletes will feel pressured to take them if their peers or competitors take them.	The harms of steroids are exaggerated. No systematic studies about their side effects have been completed.

Should steroids be banned?

Some people believe that if we changed the rules and legalized the use of steroids in sports, many of the concerns about their unfairness and even some of their harms would go away. Here are some arguments for and against lifting the ban on steroids:

Steroid use should be legalized	Steroid use should be banned
Reduce enforcement costs	
Allowing steroid use without a prescription would eliminate the high costs of enforcing drug laws.	Is it more important to lower costs or ensure safety and fairness for all athletes? If we could save money by making stealing legal, should we do that, too?
Entertainment factor	
Performances fueled by steroids elevate sports to a more spectacular level. Fans may claim to hate steroid use, but they have flocked to stadiums when steroid use was widespread.	If steroids were legal and everyone used them, the competitive advantage would be erased. Also, a majority of fans believe that steroid use is wrong. How would they feel knowing that nearly all players were using them?
More regulation equals more safety	
Legalizing drugs would mean that government agencies could control the manufacture, sale, and safety of steroids. Doctors could also legally monitor athletes using steroids, making the process safer.	Perhaps the number of deaths from steroids hasn't been greater because the drugs are not as widespread as substances such as alcohol or heroin. Legalizing steroids would change this. No matter how closely doctors monitor steroid use, the drugs still pose major health risks.
Big brother?	
The state or sports league is overreaching by telling athletes what they can and cannot put in their bodies. What's next? Will the league enact curfews and ban other "unhealthy" activities, like eating fast food or driving fast cars?	Using steroids is like smoking. It doesn't just hurt the person doing it, it also hurts those around him or her. If one athlete takes steroids to gain an advantage, another athlete will have to take a dangerous drug to remain competitive. Athletes are forced to either harm their health or compete at a huge disadvantage.

There are good arguments to be made for both sides of the issue. For many, it boils down to the "harm" factor. Do the benefits of allowing steroids ever justify the health dangers that steroids can cause athletes?

How would you feel?

How would you feel if you won a race or tournament after taking performance-enhancing drugs? Would you feel proud of your achievement? Guilty? Afraid of being caught? After sprinting his way to a gold medal in the 1988 Olympics (see page 20), Ben Johnson barely cracked a smile. His rival, Carl Lewis, believes this was because Johnson had taken steroids and could not feel good about his accomplishments, or even responsible for them.

U.S. Olympic gold medal-winning swimmer Megan Quann believes that athletes who use performance-enhancing drugs are cheating "clean" athletes of their hopes, dreams, and dollars.

OTHER PERFORMANCE-ENHANCING DRUGS AND SUPPLEMENTS

Steroids are not the only drugs athletes take to get ahead. To avoid **detection** and to achieve different advantages, many athletes take other performance-enhancing drugs, supplements, and products.

Stimulants

When track star Ben Johnson's gold medal was taken away from him for steroid use at the 1988 Seoul Olympics (see page 20), it was given to the second-place finisher, Carl Lewis. Years later, it was revealed that Lewis had also tested positive for drugs, right before the Olympics. Along with about 100 other athletes at the Olympics, his results were simply covered up.[1] The drugs found in his system were ephedrine, pseudoephedrine, and phenylpropanolamine, all banned **stimulants**. Stimulants give athletes a boost of energy, but they also have serious side effects, including insomnia, shaking, anxiety, poor coordination, irregular heart rate, and even heart attacks.

Adderall

For children and adults with Attention Deficit Hyperactivity Disorder (ADHD) or narcolepsy (a sleep disorder), the prescription drug **Adderall** can be a lifesaver. The stimulant increases focus and concentration, which benefits users in the classroom or the office. But some students and athletes without ADHD have also found ways to obtain the drug. These students use it to study longer and harder, which gives them a competitive advantage in school. Athletes also find it helps them focus more and tire less easily.

Students are rarely suspended for using the drug, even though it is illegal without a prescription. But athletes are suspended for using the drug in competition. Many athletes think this is a double standard. Why shouldn't athletes enjoy the same advantages that students do? But others say that using the drug without a prescription is both unfair and unsafe.

Scottish skier Alain Baxter was stripped of his 2002 Olympic bronze medal after testing positive for a banned stimulant, found in the cold medicine he was taking. The Court of Arbitration ruled that even accidental use of a banned substance cannot be excused.

It is possible that you have taken a stimulant of some kind, since they include caffeine and some ingredients found in common cold medicines. In fact, until 2004, the International Olympic Committee (IOC) banned large doses of caffeine. The committee finally lifted the ban so that athletes could enjoy recreational beverages like coffee or soda.

The fact that many cold medicines contain stimulants makes banning these ingredients tricky. Lewis claimed that he was taking the stimulants to treat a cold, although many doubt his story. In some cases, however, it has turned out, too late, that athletes were telling the truth when they made similar claims.

Scottish skier Alain Baxter was stripped of his 2002 bronze medal for using Vicks inhaler, a medicine used to clear sinuses. He was later cleared of wrongdoing, but he never reclaimed his medal. Romanian gymnast Andreea Raducan was stripped of a gold medal at the 2000 Sydney Olympics when she tested positive for a substance found in a cold remedy prescribed by her doctor. The amount found in her body was equivalent to one over-the-counter cold tablet.[2] As more athletes have been suspended for use of stimulants, they have become more careful about what they put in their bodies.

Increasing oxygen: Blood doping

In just 13 months from 2003 to 2004, eight top cyclists between the ages of 16 and 35 died of heart attacks. Four of them were under 24.[3] These numbers are well above average for anyone in this age group, and especially for extremely fit athletes.

Although it is hard to prove, many people believe that these cyclists were guilty of **blood doping**, the practice of increasing the number of red blood cells in the bloodstream. Increasing red blood cells increases the amount of oxygen carried to the athlete's muscles and lungs, which improves **stamina**. Athletes in sports such as cycling, long-distance running, and cross-country skiing find this especially helpful. Athletes increase their red blood cell counts in several ways, such as EPO, transfusions, or adjusting intake of oxygen.

EPO

Erythropoietin (EPO) is a synthetic substance that makes blood thicker and increases red blood cells. But EPO also makes it harder for blood to circulate, which can cause blood clotting, high blood pressure, stroke, and heart attacks. It was banned by the WADA in the early 1990s after 20 Belgian and Dutch cyclists died from unexplained heart attacks over a three-year period.[4]

EPO has proven difficult to test for, since the evidence of EPO in urine can disappear just a few days after injection—even though the effects of the drug can linger for weeks. But the WADA has recently announced an effective test for EPO, which may cut back use among athletes. Unfortunately, the extreme dangers of the drugs alone have not stopped athletes from using it.

Just say "Neigh!"

Humans are not the only ones taking performance-enhancing drugs to get ahead. Racehorses have also been given drugs. After a race in 2009, a horse belonging to the British queen tested positive for tranexamic acid, a banned substance that prevents hemorrhaging (blood loss), a common problem for young horses in competition. The queen, who was cleared of any responsibility for the scandal, called the discovery "very disappointing."[5]

Quarterback Tim Tebow uses a low-oxygen chamber after games for up to 90 minutes.

Transfusions

Athletes who don't want to risk a positive EPO test sometimes take matters into their own hands. They draw a pint or two of their own blood, which they put in storage for several weeks. On the day of competition, they transfuse the blood into their bodies, to benefit from the extra red blood cells. Blood doping of this nature is extremely hard to test for, since athletes are using their own blood, rather than a synthetic substance. But the dangers of clotting, stroke, and heart attack remain.

Low-oxygen chamber

To prepare for competitions, some top athletes, including Denver Broncos quarterback Tim Tebow, don't sleep in a normal bedroom.[6] Instead, they sleep in a tiny tent known as a low-oxygen chamber. Also called high-altitude chambers, these rooms contain a very low supply of oxygen, much like air at the top of a high mountain. Over time, the thin air forces the lung cavity to expand and absorb oxygen more efficiently. Believed to help athletes increase their **endurance**, low-oxygen training facilities have been built for athletes in Colorado and Balewadi, India.

The WADA has not banned the chambers, which many athletes find inconsistent and unfair. While EPO and blood transfusions are relatively inexpensive, oxygen chambers are expensive and hard to find. But others argue that the effectiveness of the chambers has not been proven.

Masking pain

Athletes face a lot of pressure to stay in the game after injury. Sometimes their career depends on not missing games, or a championship rides on their ability to get back on the field. Often these injured players are injected with cortisone, a powerful steroid that kills pain and decreases joint inflammation. Cortisone may get the player through the game, but the pressure the athlete puts on the injury often prevents full healing, or it even worsens the injury. This can cause long-term damage. One study showed that people who received cortisone shots had a much lower rate of full recovery than those who did nothing or underwent physical therapy. They also had a 63 percent higher risk of relapse.[7]

Several athletes have even successfully sued their teams later in life for irreversible injuries they developed when their team doctors masked their pain, instead of properly treating their condition. Team doctors, who are paid by the sports leagues, often feel pressure from their teams to "patch up," rather than heal, athletes—putting the team's interest ahead of the athlete's own well-being.

Nutritional supplements

Enter any grocery or health food store, and you will find walls of nutritional supplements: vitamins, minerals, herbs, and oils, all claiming to have amazing health and energy-boosting benefits. They seem to offer athletes safe, performance-enhancing alternatives to drugs. But do they?

In many countries, there is little regulation of the nutritional supplement industry. Most supplement manufacturers do not need to prove their products are safe or effective. Instead, it is up to government agencies to prove that they are unsafe or ineffective.[8] Some nutritional supplements are banned in sports, while others are not, which many find very confusing.

Some nutritional supplements are also contaminated with banned substances. For instance, the banned substance nandrolone has been found in vitamins and energy drinks. Canadian-born British tennis star Greg Rusedski joined a long list of athletes testing positive for the drug after taking a dietary supplement. Athletes must take these supplements at their own risk.

Manufacturers claim that nutritional supplements such as zinc, vitamin E, and calcium provide athletes with strength and energy-boosting benefits. But they are not required to provide proof for these claims.

Drugs in other professions

Drug use is not unique to sports. For example, many concert musicians calm their nerves for performances by taking different legal drugs. Why are drugs allowed in this and other occupations, but not in sports?

Some people say drug use in this example is also unacceptable—that part of being a concert musician is learning how to steady your nerves. Others argue that playing in a concert is not a competition, and that the drugs do not enhance the skills most needed for the job. For instance, a musician's most important skill is playing an instrument, not remaining calm in front of a crowd. In sports, drugs enhance the athlete's ability to perform the most essential functions of the sport, like running or jumping.

We love them and hate them

Westerners seem to have a love–hate relationship with drugs. We develop them to treat every possible ailment, but we also regard them as an "easy way out," especially in sports. Perhaps the controversy over drug use in sports is an attempt to keep sports special—one realm of society that still celebrates hard work, individual skill, and the mastery of the human body and mind. But in truth, drugs are not a magic cure-all for anything in life. Hard work and discipline are required for most accomplishments.

DRUG TESTING

In 1978 Belgian cyclist Michel Pollentier cruised to victory in the first leg of the Tour de France bicycle race. Shortly afterward, authorities stopped him at a checkpoint for drug testing, only to discover that he was hiding a pear-shaped tube of urine under his armpit. Pollentier had planned to use this "clean" urine to help him pass a drug test.[1] He was disqualified from the race, and his career never recovered.

Many other athletes have tried this and countless other methods to avoid testing positive for drugs. While drug testing seems like the fairest way to limit the use of performance-enhancing drugs in sports, drug testing authorities face many practical and ethical challenges.

Drug test challenges

Since most performance-enhancing drugs are illegal, there is a large **black market** for steroids and other drugs. Black-market operators invest large sums of money into developing new drugs that cannot be detected by current drug tests, and in developing **masking agents** (see below) that make drugs undetectable. This forces drug-testing agencies to constantly play catch-up with the dealers, in order to detect the new drugs or methods of deception.

The **human growth hormone (HGH)**, a hormone used to stimulate growth and cell production, was once used by many athletes as an alternative to steroids. They used it because it was hard to detect in drug tests. But in 2004 an effective test was finally found—and in 2010 British rugby player Terry Newton became the first athlete to officially test positive for HGH.[2]

Hiding the evidence

Masking agents are products used to conceal the detection of illegal substances in urine samples. They are banned in all kinds of drug tests. Athletes also use **diuretics**, drugs that increase the rate of urination, in an attempt to flush banned drugs out of their systems more quickly.

Most steroids are taken in four- to six-week cycles, which means athletes take the drug for four to six weeks, then let their body rest for four to six weeks. If athletes know when they will be tested, they can stop using their steroid in time to get it out of their system.

In hopes of catching athletes off-guard, authorities are instituting more random drug tests. But athletes try to get around the random tests by taking steroid pills, rather than injections, since pills exit their bodies more quickly. Unfortunately, steroid pills are also much more harmful than injections. This is because the pills pass through the liver, which can cause serious damage.

After tampering with her drug test, Irish Olympic gold-medalist Michelle Smith was allowed to keep her Olympic medals, but the ban effectively ended her career.

Michelle Smith and masking agents

In 1993 Irish swimmer Michelle Smith was ranked 90th in the world. Just three years later, she swam her way to three gold medals and a bronze in the 1996 Atlanta Olympics. Many were suspicious of her quick rise to fame, but she always tested negative for performance-enhancing substances.

In 1998, when two drug testers showed up at her house to test her, she was wearing a bulky sweater that hid much of her body as she gave her urine sample. When her sample was examined in the lab, it contained a level of alcohol that would have been deadly if consumed by a human. Smith had apparently hidden a jar of whiskey under her sweater and added the liquid to her urine as a masking agent. She was suspended for four years.[3]

Drug testing also raises many ethical concerns. Among them are the following.

Guilty until proven innocent?

In most countries, the law presumes citizens to be innocent unless proven guilty. By requiring athletes to take drug tests to prove they are innocent and suspending those who refuse, are we assuming the opposite?

How much is too much?

Athletes taking steroids can still pass drug tests. To fail a steroid test, athletes must have four times the normal amount of testosterone in their urine.[4] Drug testers allow this high maximum amount to account for any natural variations athletes might have in their testosterone levels. But this also means that an athlete could be injecting steroids without being disqualified. At the same time, even a tiny amount of other performance-enhancing drugs leads to a failed drug test.

Cross-contamination

Since some of the ingredients contained in dietary supplements are not labeled, athletes have unknowingly ingested banned substances when taking supplements. Many have been suspended from competition because of this. Some say that athletes should not be held responsible for these unlabeled ingredients. But others, including some athletes, say that "**cross-contamination**" is simply the cry of cheaters everywhere.

Privacy rights

When you imagine the glamorous lifestyle of a top athlete, you probably don't picture drug testers bursting into their homes on a vacation and following them into the bathroom. Yet, under the World Anti-**Doping** Program, this is a way of life for many athletes. A large group of athletes from every country are subject to Registered Training Pool (RTP) rules, in which they are randomly drug tested, even when not in competition. These athletes must submit information about where they will be every hour of every day, so that an Anti-Doping Authority can always locate them. When the tests are conducted, Anti-Doping personnel stay with the athlete the entire time, even while the sample is collected. If an athlete refuses or misses the doping test three times, he or she will receive the same penalty as athletes who fail a drug test.[5]

Many believe that this testing process violates an athlete's privacy rights. In 2009 the International Rowing Foundation wrote an open letter to the WADA to appeal the rules, arguing that it causes athletes undue stress and anxiety.[6] Some say that more athletes haven't spoken up for their rights because they are afraid it will make them appear guilty. On the other hand, U.S. gold medal–winning swimmers Gary Hall, Jr., and Megan Quann, who have been tested as many as 20 to 30 times a year, say that they do not mind the tests at all, since they are necessary to ensure drug-free competition. In 1995, the U.S. Supreme Court ruled that drug tests do not violate the Constitution.[7]

Alberto Contador and cross-contamination

In 2010, three-time Tour de France–winning Spanish cyclist Alberto Contador tested positive for the drug clenbuterol. He defended himself by claiming that he ate some tainted beef that contained traces of the drug. But WADA officials visited the slaughterhouse where Contador's beef was produced and found no evidence of clenbuterol use. If Contador cannot prove his innocence, he may face a two-year suspension and have his 2010 Tour de France title taken away.[8]

After testing positive for a banned substance, Tour de France winner Alberto Contador blamed it on contaminated beef. If his claim is found false, he could be stripped of his title.

YOUTH SPORTS: ROBBING THE CRADLE

On May 15, 2010, a group of eight- to ten-year-olds is playing a soccer game at the Fruitport Soccer Club in Muskegon, Michigan, when the assistant coach takes over. Within minutes, he starts screaming at the kids to run faster, and he curses at them when they miss a pass or a kick. When a parent confronts him, the coach pulls out a pistol from under his clothes, points it at the parent, and threatens to shoot.[1]

Just as professional athletes are facing increasing pressure to run faster, jump higher, and become stronger, many children are feeling it, too. Although cases like the one above are extreme—and rare—they point to the growing pressure that children face from parents and coaches to gain a competitive advantage. Some youth sports leagues even have "parent-free" zones, so that children—and their coaches—do not have to see or hear parents pressuring them from the sidelines.

Sports and fitness can be healthy for young people, and they even help prevent problems like childhood obesity (being very overweight) and depression. Sports can also teach children about teamwork, discipline, and fair play. But these positive messages are often drowned out by other, more destructive ones from parents, coaches, and the media. Are children encouraged to gain a competitive advantage too young? And at what cost?

"Scoring the 10.00 was the biggest moment for me, but at the time I didn't realize how big it was, and how everything was going to change after that. I was just a kid, I wanted to go home!"

Olympic gold medal–winning gymnast Nadia Comaneci, on scoring a perfect "10" at the age of 14, in 1976[2]

Youth in the spotlight

Six tiny, smiling girls stand on the podium at the 2008 Beijing Olympics, with gold medals draped around their necks. China's women's gymnastics team won the gold medal. But many believe that China also altered birth certificates and official records so that underage gymnasts—some as young as 13—could compete. Younger gymnasts are frequently more desirable because they are lighter, more flexible, and often more fearless when they perform difficult tricks. But athletes must be at least 16 years old to compete in Olympic gymnastics.

In the future, young Olympic-bound athletes will take bone age-assessment tests to prove they are eligible—and show six forms of identification. But should a bone assessment test be necessary to prevent adults from breaking the rules and pressuring young people to win more games or medals? What message does this send to children? That winning is everything?[3]

The Chinese women's gymnastics team won the Olympic gold medal in 2008. But these tiny girls are hardly "women." Many believe they are too young to legally compete.

Sports and education

As professional sports become a bigger and bigger business, many leagues have started extending the length of sports seasons to increase profits and television coverage. This requires athletes to train harder and play longer than ever before, something that children must also do to prepare for the big leagues.

School sports: Too much, too soon?

The emphasis on increased performance at a young age has changed the way that sports are played at many high schools and even junior highs. It has also led to the following issues:[4]

- *Serious injuries*: There has been a dramatic increase in the kinds of injuries previously seen only at the professional level. For instance, U.S. teenagers have had four times as many elbow reconstruction surgeries over the past 15 years. Concussions from football and soccer injuries are often ignored by players who want more "play time" and by coaches who want to keep their best players in the game.
- *Heavy lifting*: To "bulk up" for the professional leagues, many teenagers have engaged in weight-training programs that are too intense for growing children.
- *Focus on one sport*: In the past, teenagers often played multiple sports. But as seasons and practice sessions—as well as performance expectations—grow, many children only have time to focus on one sport. This can result in the overuse of certain muscles.

The game of life

In the past, many U.S. athletes were signed by professional teams after playing in college. Now, some leagues sign players after only a year or two in college, or even straight from high school. In Australia, athletes are often groomed for particular sports at early ages and then signed as teenagers. In Britain, athletes—especially soccer players—are often signed by sports clubs when they are as young as 16.

Many young athletes believe that sports will help them get a better life. They stake everything on this hope, while neglecting their studies in the process. One professional football player says that only 1 out of 3 of his teammates can understand the team playbook because their reading skills are so poor.[5]

Unfortunately, the odds of actually making it as a professional athlete are tiny. On average, only between 0.03 percent and 0.5 percent of high school athletes worldwide will ever go "pro."[6] For athletes who have neglected their education to focus on sports, it can be devastating to miss the cut.

The pressures of going pro so early raise a lot of ethical questions. What will these teenagers' lives be like after their professional career is over? Or what happens if they never make it big in the first place? At 16, are these athletes able to make their own life choices—or are parents, coaches, and leagues choosing their lives and careers for them?

On the other hand, some people argue that athletes have a limited window of opportunity and need to focus on sports while they are still in their physical prime. They will have time and perhaps money to finish their education after they finish their sports career. Others argue that the social and intellectual skills learned at school contribute to an athlete's maturity and abilities on the field as well as off.

These young people may already be feeling the pressure to succeed in sports. Should athletes focus solely on sports or make sure they study hard too?

Where are they now?

The pressures teenagers face can take their toll. Many young stars—both in the entertainment and the sports worlds—have made headlines later in life for arrests from drug abuse, violence, and other problems.

Andre Agassi

U.S. tennis superstar Andre Agassi was the fourth child of a father determined to make one of his kids a tennis champion. Andre was his last chance. His father fed him a drug called Excedrin—known for its high levels of caffeine—and drilled him never to be beaten. Says Agassi: "The truth is that I was in a life I didn't choose."[7] At the age of 27, Agassi finally chose to play tennis on his own terms. That is when he won five of his eight major tournaments.

Erica Blasberg

U.S. golfer Erica Blasberg's father, Mel, coached her from the time she was a little girl. In his own words, he "force-fed" her into becoming a competitor. At age 19, Blasberg became a pro golfer with sponsorships from multiple clothing companies. But then her life fell apart. She began rebelling against her father by performing and behaving badly on the course. In 2010, at the age of 25, she killed herself. Her father says, "She was forced into something she never would have done herself. Even though she didn't want to do it, she got so good, she didn't have any other choice. It was like she was trapped in her own life. Did I push her too hard? That question will haunt me for the rest of my life."[8]

Erica Blasberg turned professional in 2004. Blasberg (seen here in 2009) found the pressure of playing professional sports too much.

Christy Henrich and Allie Outram

At the age of 17, U.S. gymnast Christy Henrich was a promising contender for the Olympic team. That is when an international judge told her that she was "too fat." Her coach agreed. At first, Henrich started counting calories. Then, she began cutting them out altogether. Her unhealthy eating habits soon developed into full-blown **anorexia nervosa**, an eating disorder that leads people to starve themselves. At one point, Henrich weighed only 49 pounds (22 kilograms). She died at age 22 from multiple organ system failure.[9]

Many young top female athletes face similar pressure from coaches to lose weight, even when they are already dangerously thin. British runner Allie Outram was once bound for the Olympics. But after suffering from multiple eating disorders, she could no longer compete. She watched the 2008 Olympics from her couch.[10]

Danny Cipriani

Danny Cipriani was touted as England's next great rugby player when he was only 17. Unfortunately, he went on to disappoint many on the field and became a target of many tabloid newspapers for his colorful off-field romances. He has also battled depression. In 2010 he joined an Australian team. Some believe this was his way to escape from Britain's harsh media coverage.[11]

Danny Cipriani played rugby for London Wasps and England before moving to Australia to play for a club there.

Lessons learned

Of course, there are also plenty of young superstars who have gone on to live happy, healthy lives. But many of the athletes who have been most successful in sports and life have one thing in common—they have been driven by their own dreams and needs, not by those of their parents, coaches, or the media.

FUTURE SPORTS: DESIGNER GENES

Swedish scientist and exercise physiologist Per-Olof Åstrand said: "The most important thing an aspiring athlete can do is to choose the right parents."[1] Seven-time Tour de France-winning U.S. cyclist Lance Armstrong certainly did that. He was blessed with genes that gave him a heart one-third larger than the average man's and an endurance level almost twice that of the average person.[2] Not every athlete is blessed with such wonderful genes, but new developments in gene technology may soon make it possible for athletes—or their parents—to select genes that could give them a competitive edge.

Visions of the future

The year is 2025, and an army of 20 athletes stands at the starting line of the marathon. The gun goes off, and so do the runners. After only 1 mile (1.6 kilometers), 19 of the runners have pulled way ahead, leaving one runner in the dust. After 26 miles (42 kilometers), the 19 runners finish within minutes of one another. But the last runner takes twice as long to struggle to the finish line. Why is the final runner so slow? He is the only runner whose genes have not been enhanced. If he had competed in the 2015 marathon, he would have won the race!

Of course, this future may not come to pass. But we will likely have the technology to make it possible. For mice, we already do. Scientists discovered a gene in mice they call a "fat switch." Whenever this gene was turned on, the mice burned fat, which gave them a steady supply of energy. Scientists then changed the genes of the mice so that the "fat switch gene" was always turned on. When placed on a treadmill, these "marathon mice" ran twice as far as regular mice before stopping. If applied in the future to humans, this "fat switch" gene technology could transform average athletes into super-marathon runners.[3]

Gene therapy

To put these genetic discoveries to use in humans, scientists would need to perform **gene therapy**, a method of replacing existing genes with new ones. In 1999 gene therapy was successfully performed on two French infants suffering from Severe Combined Immunodeficiency (SCID), a genetic immune system disorder.

But the procedure worried scientists. The boys were cured of SCID, but both became sick with leukemia, a cancer of the blood. Although the cancer was successfully treated, many believe that doctors still do not know enough to safely perform gene therapy on humans. But as scientists learn more, gene therapy may become commonplace for treating diseases. Some scientists believe it will only be a matter of time before gene therapy is used to help athletes become bigger or stronger.

Rhys Evans was the first British infant to receive gene therapy for SCID, an immune deficiency disorder. Some predict that athletes will someday use this method to create bigger muscles.

Superstrength

It's a bird, it's a plane, it's Super Boy! In Berlin, Germany, there is a four-year-old boy so strong he can hold 7-pound (3-kilogram) weights with his arms fully extended, like Superman, something many adults cannot do. He has muscles twice as large as most children his age and only half the body fat. The reason for his super-human strength is a rare genetic mutation that keeps his myostatin gene (a protein that limits muscle growth) permanently turned off. With the gene shut off, muscles grow twice as fast. If information about this mutation is applied to athletes, it could make them incredibly strong.[4]

Ethics of gene enhancement

Using gene therapies to enhance performance raises many ethical concerns. Some groups object to the idea because they believe that nature, not humans, should determine a child's genetic makeup. Others are more concerned about the safety and fairness of using genetic methods to create "super-jocks."

Most scientists agree that gene enhancement therapies are still unsafe for humans. Scientists need to learn more about this branch of science. Like cosmetic surgery, which is performed for beauty rather than medical reasons, genetic enhancement would use medical methods for non-medical purposes—like growing bigger muscles. This could put athletes at unnecessary risk. But that may not stop some athletes.

Leveling the playing field?

Life is not always fair. Some children are good at sports, while others are not. Would it make sense, then, to use genetic enhancement to help "level the playing field" for children who lack athletic ability? Some people say that genetics have always been like a lottery, or the luck of the draw. Gene enhancement would provide children who are unlucky in sports a better baseline to compete.

Others argue that a level playing field is exactly what we don't want. If everyone performs better, then no single person performs better. Plus, a level playing field would only be available to those whose parents could afford expensive gene therapies. Rather than turning children who are not good at sports into athletes, perhaps we should encourage them to develop their own unique gifts. An emphasis on sports might even prevent them from becoming a world-famous painter, author, or doctor.

Gene doping

In anticipation of a new generation of genetically modified athletes, the WADA has already banned "**gene doping**," or genetic enhancement, among athletes. They have also discovered a blood test that can accurately determine whether a person has been genetically altered.[5] But their rule raises questions. For example, should athletes whose parents selected their traits be punished for their parents' decisions?

Build a baby

What if parents could choose traits for their children from a giant shopping list? They could chose eye color, height, flexibility, muscle size, or maybe even a talent for music or sports. With gene enhancement technology, this could become a reality.

But should we allow parents to do this? Many people are strongly opposed to the idea. They claim that some parents might select traits in their children as a way to fulfill their own dreams, instead of allowing their children to develop dreams of their own. Also shouldn't parents unconditionally love their children, instead of demanding "perfection," or a certain body type?

Others say that parents already influence their children heavily. They feed them certain foods, take them to certain classes, and offer them certain opportunities to get ahead. They also provide kids half of their own genes. Genetic enhancement, they argue, would just be another way for parents to influence their children.

But others argue that genetic selection would only increase the pressure parents already place on children. For instance, how would you feel if you learned you had been "designed" by your parents to be a golfer? What if you would rather do something else with your life? What if you weren't good at golf? Would you see yourself as a failure? Would your parents?

How much control should parents have over their children's traits? Should athletes be allowed to alter their own genes with gene enhancement therapies?

EXTREME SPORTS AND THE NEXT GENERATION

In 1999 U.S. skateboarding legend Tony Hawk accomplished something no one had ever done before: a 900 (two-and-a-half rotation aerial spin) in competition. Footage of the X Games shows Hawk attempting the trick over and over as the crowd chants his name. The other skaters bang their skateboards in support. And the announcers let Hawk continue trying, even after time has officially expired. When Hawk finally lands the trick, on his 11th attempt, the other skaters mob him and hoist him into the air.[1]

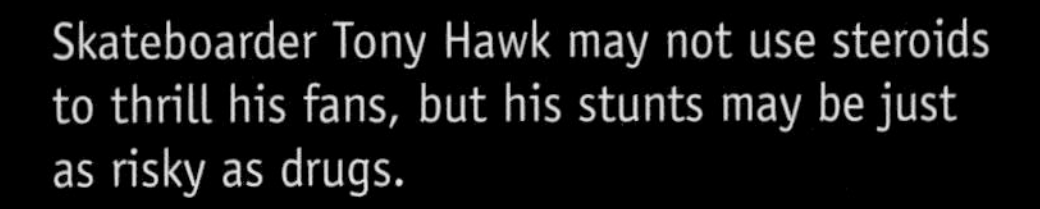

Skateboarder Tony Hawk may not use steroids to thrill his fans, but his stunts may be just as risky as drugs.

In the past 20 years, extreme sports such as skateboarding, snowboarding, and motocross have exploded in popularity, especially among young people. That is about the same time period when steroid use exploded in traditional sports. Some people think there is a connection between the two. Many people, especially the younger generation, are disgusted with the "win at all costs" attitude on display in many traditional sports. They are looking for something new and different.

Tony Hawk's amazing moment captures the essence of many extreme sports: the excitement of inventing new tricks, the sense of support among opponents, and the looseness of rules. Here are some other differences between traditional sports (such as soccer, football, cricket, and tennis) and newer, extreme sports:

Traditional sports	Extreme sports
Many records have already been set. To break new records, many athletes believe they need to use steroids.	Since the sports are still young, there is more potential for achievement. New moves are invented and records are frequently broken, with no need for performance-enhancing drugs.
Many athletes use performance-enhancing drugs to remain physically competitive in terms of speed, strength, and endurance.	Performances in extreme sports often rely not so much on strength and speed alone, but rather on daring, intelligence, creativity, and flexibility.
The rules of the game have been long established. Unfortunately, so has cheating!	Athletes rarely cheat because there are few rules. Athletes tend to make up rules as they go along, which keeps the sport changing and interesting.
New technology is often embraced very slowly. Some people feel it offers an unfair advantage and makes the game too easy.	New technology is embraced. New innovations allow athletes to attempt even greater challenges and more amazing feats.
Winning is the main focus. The whole point is to defeat opponents.	The point is to push personal limits, to thrill oneself and one's fans—and to have fun. Competitors help, inspire, and instruct.
Many young people are harmed by the stresses involved in making it to the top.	Many extreme sport athletes go "pro" at young ages, but there are far fewer stories of lives gone wrong.

Extreme drawbacks

Part of the excitement of extreme sports lies in their newness. Athletes are still making up moves. But in 20 years, new moves may be harder to come by and records may be harder to break. As extreme sports become more established, they will probably have more rules and regulations. Also, the cost of the technologies needed to compete may leave a lot of people behind. For instance, two-time Olympic gold medal–winning snowboarder Shaun White practices on a private half-pipe in his backyard, something most people cannot afford.

Sports psychology: The power of the mind

At one time, running a mile in less than four minutes seemed like an impossible feat. Then, in 1954, a runner named Roger Bannister did it.[2] Pretty soon, other runners did, too. Did they all simply have better shoes, diets, or drugs than runners in 1953? Or did Bannister break a **psychological** as well as physical barrier when he proved what was possible?

In most sports, once a feat has been accomplished, the way is paved for others to follow. How do athletes always seem to catch up? Perhaps the very nature of competition raises the bar on performance.

Fortunately, physics tells us that there is a lot yet to accomplish in sports. For instance, scientists say that athletes have yet to hit the longest home run that it is physically possible for the human body to hit—even without steroids.[3] Scientists also believe that it is physically possible for humans to survive a quadruple flip on a motorcycle.[4] So far, no one has accomplished more than a double. Performing these feats is a question of nerve, skill, and imagination—not drugs or technology.

Scientists say that humans should be able to perform a quadruple flip on a motorcycle, even if it seems impossible now.

Placebo effect

Since 2007 athletes such as Kobe Bryant, Shaquille O'Neal, and David Beckham have sported Power Balance bracelets. Power Balance has claimed that these rubberized bands improve balance, strength, and flexibility. But tests have shown that athletes wearing them perform no better than athletes wearing plain rubber bracelets.[5]

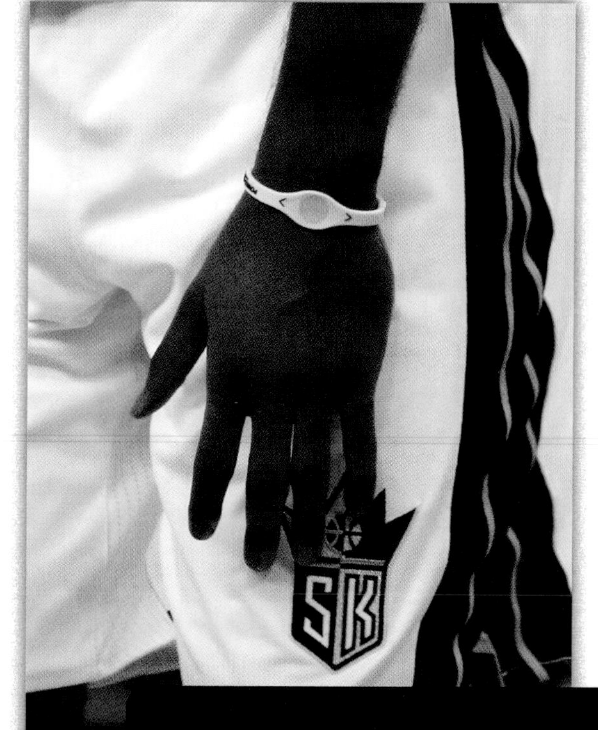

Some athletes believe that wearing Power Balance bracelets will help them to perform well.

But the power of belief is strong. If athletes believe that a lucky bracelet or a lucky shirt helps them play better, the belief itself could give them the confidence to make it happen. This is what is known as a **placebo effect**, in which people experience genuine improvement from a fake treatment—or an object with no real power—simply because they believe it will help.

Some people believe that many so-called performance-enhancing drugs might operate on this principle, too. For instance, many people believe that HGH contributes only minimally, if at all, to a player's performance.[6] They argue that an athlete's belief in the pill's effectiveness motivates him or her to work harder and perform better (see the box below).

Richard Sandlin and the placebo effect

Weightlifter Richard Sandlin took steroids for many years, even though he developed many negative side effects. Eventually he stopped taking them—and he surprised himself by setting six new world records in power lifting. That is when he learned the importance of mental strength in the sport. While physical strength is important to weightlifting, so is focusing energy at precisely the right moments. He believes now that he took the steroids as a substitute for confidence.[7]

TOPICS FOR DISCUSSION

The following are some more ethical issues in sports for you to think about and discuss with your classmates.

Faking it

It is September 15, 2010, and Tampa Bay Rays relief pitcher Chad Qualls winds up his pitch to Yankees shortstop Derek Jeter. As the ball sails toward the plate, Jeter grabs his elbow and howls in apparent pain. The home plate umpire sends Jeter to first base, for being hit by the ball. But instant replays later show that the ball did not, in fact, hit Jeter. Jeter faked the whole thing. Some fans branded him "Jeter Cheater," but Jeter defended his move. He said, "What am I supposed to say [to the umpire]? 'Sorry sir, but it didn't hit me, please let me continue to hit?'"[1]

But there is a difference between not correcting an incorrect call and faking injury in hopes of drawing the wrong call. Did Jeter cross the line? Some say that deceiving an official to get on base is never acceptable. Others say that "play-acting" is an expected part of the game—and Jeter behaved no differently than batters who dramatically duck away from pitches that come nowhere near them. There are a lot of rules in baseball, but "no faking" is not one of them.

But "faking" is against the rules in other sports—sort of. FIFA (the international organization that regulates soccer) has made it illegal in soccer to deceive the referee by faking injury or a foul, a practice commonly called "diving." The punishment is a yellow card, or warning. But in reality, it is very hard for referees to spot the difference between real and fake fouls without instant replay to consult. Some referees say that faking must be very obvious for them to penalize it, since issuing a card is a way of accusing a player of dishonesty.[2]

Some players don't mind diving, since the calls for and against their team balance out over time. Others say that just because both sides "cheat" doesn't mean the practice is acceptable. They believe that accepting or even celebrating diving dishonors the skills soccer is supposed to promote: kicking the ball with precision and control. Most players also object to being penalized for fouling an athlete who is merely faking.

Professional basketball and hockey also have rules against faking, but they do not stop players from getting away with it. Instead of banning the practice altogether—the way that most leagues ban drugs—the organizations have a built-in penalty or punishment for faking, as if it is an expected part of the game. Some say that faking is an act of desperation—something teams do if they are down. But it takes more than faking to make up for poor play. Just ask Derek Jeter. His Yankees ended up losing to Tampa Bay 4–3.[3]

The role of role models

Basketball star Charles Barkley famously said, "I am not a role model." He suggested that parents, not athletes, should instead be role models for their kids. But fellow NBA player Karl Malone shot back by saying, "You don't choose to be a role model; you are chosen. It's not your decision to make! I try to be a positive one."[4] Who is right?

Whether they like it or not, superstars do influence many teenagers who look up to athletes bigger, stronger, and richer than themselves. Many teenagers want to look like and act like their heroes. While most superstars would never advise children to take steroids, many use steroids themselves—a message that many teenagers notice. In fact, if a top athlete tests positive for a steroid, sales for that particular drug go way up. The athlete has just proved it is effective.[5]

What do you think? Should sportspeople think about the effect their actions might have on their fans?

GLOSSARY

Adderall prescription stimulant that increases focus and concentration. It is used primarily for those with Attention Deficit Hyperactivity Disorder (ADHD) or narcolepsy, a sleep disorder.

aerodynamic designed with smooth surfaces or rounded edges in order to reduce drag from wind on an object

anabolic steroid synthetic (made in a laboratory) hormone used to cause muscle growth. It is legal only with a prescription in most countries.

anorexia nervosa eating disorder characterized by a refusal to maintain a healthy body weight and an obsessive fear of gaining weight

biomechanics science of applying the laws of mechanics to the human body in order to gain a greater understanding of athletic performance

black market underground or illegal market for products that are unlawful or stolen

blood doping practice of increasing the number of red blood cells in the bloodstream, to increase their ability to carry oxygen and improve athletic performance

concussion injury to the brain caused by a violent blow or harsh impact

cortisone steroid that treats illnesses or injuries by reducing inflammation and pain at the site of the injury

cross-contamination passing of a harmful substance from one person or thing to another

detection process of discovering something that has been hidden

diuretic substance or drug that tends to increase the rate of urination

doping use of a drug or blood product to improve athletic performance

endurance ability to withstand physical or mental difficulty over a prolonged period

erythropoietin (EPO) synthetic substance that makes blood thicker and increases red blood cells

ethical relating to ethics, or issues of right and wrong

ethics rules or standards of conduct for a person or the members of a profession

gene unit consisting of a sequence of DNA; it determines a particular trait in an organism

gene doping manipulation of genes, with the intention of improving athletic performance

gene therapy method of replacing damaged genes by inserting healthy genes into human cells

hormone chemical substance produced in the body that regulates certain cells or organs

human growth hormone (HGH) natural or synthetically generated hormone used to stimulate growth and cell production in humans

infertile unable to become pregnant or reproduce

insomnia consistent inability to fall asleep

invincible incapable of being injured or defeated; unconquerable

ligament sheet or band of tough tissue that connects bones or cartilage at a joint

masking agent product used to conceal the detection of illegal substances in urine samples

media collective name for different means of communication, such as newspapers, television, and the Internet

nutritional supplement vitamin, herb, mineral, or sports-nutrition food or beverage used to boost the immune system or improve athletic and mental performance

paralysis inability to move. Paralysis can be temporary or permanent.

patent to have exclusive rights to make or sell an idea or invention

performance-enhancing drug substance used by athletes to improve their performance in sports

placebo effect phenomenon of a patient experiencing a beneficial effect from a treatment, even if the treatment is fake, simply because the patient expects a positive outcome

psychological mental or emotional, rather than physical

rugby rugby union is a game played by two teams of 15 players, popular in many countries around the world

sponsor pay money to support something. Companies may sponsor an athlete or event as a form of advertising. The word is also used to describe the person or company doing the sponsoring.

stamina ability to sustain physical or mental effort for a long period of time

steroid kind of drug taken by some athletes to improve their performance

stimulant any chemical that temporarily increases activity in the central nervous system (brain and spinal cord) or cardiovascular system. Stimulants generally increase alertness, heart rate, breathing rate, blood pressure, and energy level.

synthetic substance that is produced artificially, in a laboratory or other human-made environment

testosterone male sex hormone responsible for the growth of the male reproductive organs as well as muscles and bone mass

unethical relating to behavior considered morally wrong

World Anti-Doping Agency (WADA) independent agency that coordinates the fight against the improper use of drugs and performance-enhancing substances in sports

NOTES ON SOURCES

HIGHER! FASTER! STRONGER! (pages 4–7)

1. The Olympic Museum, "The Olympic Symbols," http://www.olympic.org/Documents/Reports/EN/en_report_1303.pdf.
2. Martin Hollis, *Trust Within Reason* (Cambridge University Press, 1998), 106.

TECHNOLOGY: A GAME CHANGER (pages 8–19)

1. Alex Altman, "The World's Fastest Human," *Time*, August 18, 2009, http://www.time.com/time/arts/article/0,8599,1917099,00.html.
2. Altman, "The World's Fastest Human."
3. Ralf Jarkowski, "The Day Jesse Owens Bettered Five Records and Tied Another," *The Earth Times*, May 24, 2010, http://www.earthtimes.org/articles/news/325208,the-day-jesse-owens-bettered-five-records-and-tied-another.html.
4. Robin Finn, "Borg Comeback II: A Passion Play Rewritten," *New York Times*, March 1, 1992, http://www.nytimes.com/1992/03/01/sports/tennis-borg-comeback-ii-a-passion-play-rewritten.html.
5. John Branch, "Rejection by N.B.A. Gives New Shoes Even Greater Bounce," *New York Times*, October 20, 2010, http://www.nytimes.com/2010/10/21/sports/basketball/21shoes.html.
6. Branch, "Rejection by N.B.A."
7. Ron Fridell, *Sports Technology* (Minneapolis: Lerner Publications, 2009), 15.
8. John Powers, "Were Records Just Material Gains?" *Boston Globe*, August 11, 2009, http://www.boston.com/sports/other_sports/olympics/articles/2009/08/11/swimming_records_may_have_been_just_material_gains/.
9. BBC News, "High Tech Swimsuits No Longer Legal," July 31, 2009, http://news.bbc.co.uk/sport2/hi/other_sports/swimming/8161867.stm.
10. Jeff Jones and John Stevenson, "An Overview of Track Cycling," Cycling News, http://autobus.cyclingnews.com/track/?id=trackoverview00.
11. Rosemary Barnes, "UCI Says It Is Cracking Down on Track Cycling Technology," *Sports Technology Ethics: Commentary and Opinion on the Ethics of Technology in Sport*, March 20, 2010, http://sportstechethics.blogspot.com/2010/03/uci-says-it-is-cracking-down-on-track.html.
12. Barnes, "UCI Says It Is Cracking Down."
13. Barnes, "UCI Says It Is Cracking Down."
14. "New Lure's Catch Rate May Be Too High for Some Tournaments," *Outdoor Life: New Sports Technology*, 216, no. 3 (March 2009): 79.
15. Barnes, "UCI Says It Is Cracking Down."
16. Barnes, "UCI Says It Is Cracking Down."
17. *Modern Marvels Presents: Sports Technology: Equipment* (New York: A & E Home Video, 1998).
18. Stephanie Smith, "Concussions Extra Dangerous to Teen Brains," CNN, February 3, 2010, http://articles.cnn.com/2010-02-03/health/concussions.teen.brains_1_concussions-david-bosse-school?_s=PM:HEALTH.
19. Smith, "Concussions Extra Dangerous to Teen Brains."
20. Reed Albergotti and Shirley S. Wang, "Is it Time to Retire the Football Helmet?" *Wall Street Journal*, November 11, 2009, http://online.wsj.com/article/SB10001424052748704402404574527881984299454.html.

21. Albergotti and Wang, "Is it Time to Retire the Football Helmet?"
22. Joel Stein, "Stallone on a Mission," *Time*, January 24, 2008, p. 2, http://www.time.com/time/magazine/article/0,9171,1706759-2,00.html
23. *Modern Marvels Presents*.
24. Mike Slocombe, "Smartball May Help Football Goal Decisions," *Digital Lifestyles*, February 28, 2005, http://digital-lifestyles.info/2005/02/28/smartball-may-help-football-goal-decisions/.
25. Peter Singer, "Why Is Cheating O.K. in Football?" *The Guardian*, June 29, 2010, http://www.guardian.co.uk/commentisfree/2010/jun/29/cheating-football-germany-goalkeeper.

STEROIDS: IS BIGGER BETTER? (pages 20–29)

1. "Easily Obtained Steroids Focus of Debate," *Sports Illustrated*, November 26, 2003, http://sportsillustrated.cnn.com/2003/more/11/26/us.doping.ap/.
2. UK Drug Zone.com, "Steroids," http://www.ukdrugzone.com/drugs/drug_list/steroids_drugs.html.
3. Steroid-abuse.org, "Real Truth About Steroids," http://www.steroid-abuse.org/index.htm.
4. ESPN, "Anabolic Steroids," http://espn.go.com/special/s/drugsandsports/steroids.html.
5. JCSgroup.com, "Performance-Enhancers Are What the Pros Swear By—and Die By," http://www.jcs-group.com/what/lethal/wrestling.html.
6. Judy Monroe, *Steroid Drug Dangers* (Berkeley Heights, N.J.: Enslow Publishers, 1999), 15.
7. Drug Info, "Steroids: Usage Trends," http://ecstasy.com.ua/l3/steroids-usage-trends.html.
8. Rebecca Leung, "The Kid Next Door: Teen Athletes Who Use Steroids May Be at Risk," *60 Minutes*, July 21, 2004, http://www.cbsnews.com/stories/2004/03/02/60II/main603502.shtml.
9. Patrick Zickler, "NIDA Initiative Targets Increasing Teen Use of Anabolic Steroids," *National Institute on Drug Abuse* 15, no. 3 (August 2000): 12.
10. "Steroids: Usage Trends."
11. Monitoring the Future, The University of Michigan. Table 1: http://www.monitoringthefuture.org/pubs/monographs/mtf-overview2010.pdf, 46; The Home Office's British Crime Survey, Table 2.6c, http://www.ic.nhs.uk/webfiles/publications/Health%20and%20Lifestyles/sdd2009/SDD_2009_Report.pdf.
12. Jerry Crasnick, "Aaron advocates asterisks by records," July 27, 2009, ESPN Baseball Hall of Fame, 2009, http://sports.espn.go.com/mlb/hof09/news/story?id=4355886.

OTHER PERFORMANCE-ENHANCING DRUGS AND SUPPLEMENTS (pages 30–35)

1. Jacquelin Magnay, "Carl Lewis's Positive Test Covered Up," *Sydney Morning Herald*, April 18, 2003, http://www.smh.com.au/articles/2003/04/17/1050172709693.html.
2. Ash Ley, "Top 10 Olympic Athletes Who Lost Their Olympic Medals," TopTenz.net, http://www.toptenz.net/top-10-athletes-who-lost-their-olympic-medal.php.
3. William Fotheringham, "Inquiry into Belgian Cyclist's Death Raises New Fears over EPO," *The Guardian*, February 16, 2004, http://www.guardian.co.uk/sport/2004/feb/16/cycling.cycling1.
4. World Anti-Doping Agency, "EPO Q & A," http://www.wada-ama.org/en/Resources/Q-and-A/Q-A-EPO-Detection/.
5. Associated Press, "Horse Tested Positive After Debut Race," ESPN, May 8, 2009, http://sports.espn.go.com/sports/horse/news/story?id=4151479.

OTHER PERFORMANCE-ENHANCING DRUGS AND SUPPLEMENTS (pages 30–35)

6. Kent Sepkowitz, *Slate Magazine*, September 9, 2010, p.1: http://www.slate.com/id/2266601/; "Bigger, Stronger, Faster," Magnolia Home Entertainment, 2008: http://www.youtube.com/watch?v=kUYok77mMCk.
7. Gretchen Reynolds, "Phys Ed: Do Cortisone Shots Actually Make Things Worse?" *New York Times*, October 27, 2010, http://well.blogs.nytimes.com/2010/10/27/do-cortisone-shots-actually-make-things-worse/.
8. U.S. Food and Drug Administration, "Overview of Dietary Supplements," October 14, 2009, http://www.fda.gov/food/dietarysupplements/consumerinformation/ucm110417.htm.

DRUG TESTING (pages 36–39)

1. Jon Henderson, "The 10 Greatest Cheats in Sporting History," *The Guardian*, July 8, 2001, http://observer.guardian.co.uk/toptens/story/0,,1079053,00.html.
2. Jacquelin Magnay, "Terry Newton Drugs Breakthrough Prompts Human Growth Hormone Alert," *The Telegraph*, February 24, 2010, http://www.telegraph.co.uk/sport/othersports/drugsinsport/7309878/Terry-Newton-drugs-breakthrough-prompts-human-growth-hormone-alert.html.
3. Jere Longman, "Olympic Swimming Star Banned; Tampering with Drug Test Cited," *New York Times*, August 7, 1998, http://www.nytimes.com/1998/08/07/sports/swimming-olympic-swimming-star-banned-tampering-with-drug-test-cited.html.
4. Sal Rulbal, "From spotlight to suspicion: Landis' drug test a blow to cycling," July 30, 2006, http://www.usatoday.com/sports/cycling/2006-07-27-landis-drug-test_x.htm.
5. RFU, "National Registered Drug Testing Pool," 2010, http://www.rfu.com/TheGame/AntiDoping/PlayerWhereabouts/NationalTestingPool.
6. Mark Bisson, "Rowing Appeals for Changes to WADA Rule," *Around the Rings*, February 20, 2009, http://www.aroundtherings.com/articles/view.aspx?id=31547.
7. USLegal.com, "Mandatory Suspicionless Testing of Student Athletes Ruled Constitutional," http://education.uslegal.com/drug-testing-in-public-schools/federal-court-decisions/mandatory-suspicionless-testing-of-student-athletes-ruled-constitutional/.
8. Juliet Macur, "Contador Questions Process and Says He'll Appeal Ban," *New York Times*, January 28, 2011, http://www.nytimes.com/2011/01/29/sports/cycling/29cycling.html.

YOUTH SPORTS: ROBBING THE CRADLE (pages 40–45)

1. Leon Hendrix, "Assistant Coach Pulls Gun on Soccer Dad," Wood TV8.com, May 17, 2010.
2. Celia Brackenridge and Daniel Rhind, *Elite Child Athlete Welfare: International Perspectives* (London: Brunel University, 2010), 121, http://www.brunel.ac.uk/374/Sport%20Sciences%20Research%20Documents/EliteChildAthleteWelfareBook.pdf.
3. *People's Daily Online*, "Strict Measures Adopted to Keep Age Problem off Chinese Delegation," July 28, 2010, http://english.peopledaily.com.cn/90001/90779/90867/7084363.html.
4. John McCloskey and Julian Bailes, *When Winning Costs Too Much* (Lanham, MD: Taylor Trade Publishing, 2005), 190.
5. Robert L. Simon, *Fair Play: The Ethics of Sport* (Boulder, CO.: Westview Press), 2004, 145.
6. Simon, *Fair Play: The Ethics of Sport*, 149.
7. Liz Clarke, "Andre Agassi Stays Busy with Charitable Ventures after Tennis Career," *The*

Washington Post, November 15, 2010, http://www.washingtonpost.com/wp-dyn/content/article/2010/11/14/AR2010111403812.html.
8. Alan Shipnuck, "The Mystery of Erica Blasberg," *Sports Illustrated*, December 13, 2010, http://sportsillustrated.cnn.com/vault/article/magazine/MAG1179711/index.htm.
9. Brackenridge and Rhind, *Elite Child Athlete Welfare*, 120.
10. Peta Bee, "Anorexia Athletica: The Price That Many Female Athletes Pay for Gold," *The Sunday Times*, August 4, 2008, http://www.timesonline.co.uk/tol/life_and_style/health/article4445180.ece.
11. Mick Cleary, "Danny Cipriani's Exile to Australia Will Not Trouble England," *The Telegraph*, February 19, 2010, http://www.telegraph.co.uk/sport/rugbyunion/dannycipriani/7273443/Danny-Ciprianis-exile-to-Australia-will-not-trouble-England.html.

FUTURE SPORTS: DESIGNER GENES (pages 46–49)

1. Stefan Lovgren, "Olympic Gold Begins with Good Genes, Experts Say," National Geographic News, August 20, 2004, http://news.nationalgeographic.com/news/2004/08/0820_040820_olympics_athletes.html.
2. Jane Elliott, "What Makes a Great Tour Rider?" BBC News, July 6, 2007, http://news.bbc.co.uk/2/hi/6273202.stm.
3. Ron Fridell, *Genetic Engineering* (Minneapolis: Lerner Publications, 2006), 36.
4. Fridell, *Genetic Engineering*, 37.
5. Associated Press, "Gene Doping Test Developed," *New York Times*, September 4, 2010, http://www.nytimes.com/2010/09/04/sports/04sportsbriefs-genes.html.

EXTREME SPORTS AND THE NEXT GENERATION (pages 50–53)

1. Polly Sprenger, "Twist and Shout at the X Games," *Wired*, June 28, 1999.
2. Tom Michalik, "Roger Bannister Describes Breaking the Four Minute Mile Barrier," Randolph College, http://faculty.randolphcollege.edu/tmichalik/4min.htm.
3. John Brenkus, "The Longest Home Run Ever," *The Week*, October 29, 2010, http://theweek.com/article/index/208794/the-longest-home-run-ever.
4. Buzz Skyline, "Freestyle Backflip Motocross Limit," Extreme Sports Physics, July 2, 2007, http://extremesportsphysics.blogspot.com/2007/07/fmx-backflips-limit-14.html.
5. Benjamin Radford, "Power Balance Maker Admits Bands Are Worthless," Discovery News, January 10, 2011, http://news.discovery.com/human/power-balance-maker-admits-bands-are-worthless.html.
6. R. Drysdale, "Does HGH Work?" Health Guidance for Better Health, http://www.healthguidance.org/entry/5848/1/Does-HGH-Work.html.
7. Mike Reilley, "Steroids Are Risky Business," *L.A. Times*, September 12, 1990, http://articles.latimes.com/1990-09-12/sports/sp-338_1_steroid-abuse.

TOPICS FOR DISCUSSION (pages 54–55)

1. Brian Goff, "Faking=Cheating? The Curious Case of Derek Jeter," *The Christian Science Monitor*, September 21, 2010, http://www.csmonitor.com/Business/The-Sports-Economist/2010/0921/Faking-cheating-The-curious-case-of-Derek-Jeter.
2. Jeffrey Marcus, "When a Soccer Star Falls, It May Be Great Acting," The New York Times, June 20, 2010, http://www.nytimes.com/2010/06/21/sports/soccer/21diving.html.
3. ESPN, "MLB Box Scores," http://scores.espn.go.com/mlb/boxscore?gameId=300915130.
4. Simon, *Fair Play: The Ethics of Sport*, 6.

FIND OUT MORE

Books

Balcavage, Dynise. *Steroids (Junior Drug Awareness)*. Philadelphia: Chelsea House, 2000.

Fridell, Ron. *Genetic Engineering (Cool Science)*. Minneapolis: Lerner, 2006.

Fridell, Ron. *Sports Technology (Cool Science)*. Minneapolis: Lerner, 2009.

Judson, Karen. *Genetic Engineering: Debating the Benefits and Concerns (Issues in Focus)*. Berkeley Heights, N.J.: Enslow, 2001.

Parks, Peggy J. *Drugs and Sports (Current Issues)*. San Diego: Reference Point, 2010.

Santella, Thomas M. *Body Enhancement Products (Drugs: The Straight Facts)*. Philadelphia: Chelsea House, 2005.

DVDs

Chariots of Fire (Burbank, Calif.: Warner Home Video, 1981; reissued 2005).
This movie tells the story of two very different runners competing for the 1924 British Olympic team. One uses a professional trainer, while the other does not.

The Flying Scotsman (Beverly Hills, Calif.: Twentieth Century Fox Home Entertainment, 2007).
Small, scrappy bicycle store owner Graeme Obree hopes to become a professional cyclist—but he lacks the funds. So, he gets innovative and invents a more efficient bicycle using spare parts from a washing machine and sets a one-hour world record. Based on a true story.

Sports Technology: Equipment (New York: A & E Television Networks, 2008).
This documentary traces the history of sports technology from ancient times to the end of the 1900s.

New Explorers: The Science of Sports (New York: A & E Television Networks, 2008).
This movie highlights how science and technology have contributed to the evolution of performance in sports.

Rocky IV (Santa Monica, Calif.: MGM Home Entertainment, 1985; reissued 2004).
A battle between East and West ensues when U.S. boxer Rocky Balboa takes on Russian boxer "Drago." Rocky uses old-fashioned training methods, while Drago uses high-tech methods—and steroids.

Pumping Iron (New York: HBO Home Video, 1977; reissued 2003).
A movie about weightlifting and bodybuilding that introduced the world to both steroids and bodybuilder-turned-politician Arnold Schwarzenegger.

Websites

www.wada-ama.org
Visit the Word Anti-Doping Agency's official website to find the official list of prohibited substances in sports as well as useful anti-doping information and resources. Kids can visit the Youth Zone.

http://josephsoninstitute.org/sports/pvwh-sportsmanship/
Visit this fair play blog from the Josephson Institute's Center for Sports Ethics to find entertaining, timely, and true stories of sports stars from around the world who are setting good (and bad) examples in sports.

www.steroid-abuse.org/index.htm
This website was created by a group of doctors, steroid users, and experts in the field of sports. The website aims to dispel myths about steroid use, while providing comprehensive information on how to stop steroid abuse.

Suggestions for further research

- Do sports and school mix? Are sports emphasized too much at certain high schools and colleges? Do players sacrifice their educations, as indicated by the low college graduation rates of many athletes? Should elite college athletes be paid?
- Sometimes players fake injury in order to get ahead. Is this type of "intentional cheating" just an expected "part of the game," or does this kind of behavior have no place in sports?
- Is drug testing for athletes an invasion of privacy? If so, how can a drug-free sports culture be maintained? If not, is drug testing also acceptable in other professions? Which ones and why?
- What factors make modern-day players stronger or faster than athletes from previous generations? Taking these factors (diet, rule changes, drug use, equipment changes, timing methods, and training methods) into consideration, compare the statistics of an old generation and a new generation player.
- Using British diver Tom Daley as an example, review the issue of "bullying" in sports. Also examine the ethics of "hazing" in sports.
- Explore the benefits and drawbacks of running barefoot versus using state-of-the-art running shoes in recreational running.
- Discuss the issue of gene doping. Is it wrong for athletes to modify their genes? If so, why is it worse than other kinds of technologies?

INDEX